TRIUMPH

THE SAVVY YOU NEED TO
FULFILL YOUR LIFE OF PURPOSE

Akif Felix

VIDE

Vide Press
6200 Second Street
Washington D.C. 20011
www.VidePress.com

PB ISBN: 978-1-954618-43-5
eBook ISBN: 978-1-954618-44-2

Printed in the United States of America

Epigraph

"For the Spirit God gave us does not make us timid,

but gives us power, love, and self-discipline."

2 Timothy 1:7

Table of Contents

Introduction

None of us were born perfect. Chances are, you're reading this book because you are too familiar with what it is like to feel withdrawn. And, if you are a Millennial like myself, you would agree that our age group has had the harshest experience thus far coping with mental health. In our brief existence, we have experienced national mass shootings at an unreasonable rate, the terrorist attacks of September 11, 2001, innumerable record-breaking natural disasters, heightened civil unrest, and the birth and rapid growth of the internet, smartphones, and social media to magnify these devastations. Now, with the arrival of the Covid-19 pandemic, seclusion is on the rise as a result of the ensuing lockdowns and decline of social assemblies.

You are aware of how isolating, incapacitating, and exhausting life can feel at times. And if so, you're probably sick and tired of feeling this way, and with good reason. These overwhelming feelings can be hugely disruptive, especially for someone who's got big goals to accomplish and personal aspirations as you do. Between juggling work assignments, caring for your child or loved one, and finding social time, you are trying your very best. On top of that, dealing with a racing heart, intrusive thoughts, and suffocating sadness can make a lot feel like too much. Worst of all, you may be fearful to share what you're experiencing with anyone because even you, at times, have questioned the legitimacy of your experiences. In times like these, it is tempting to throw the towel in and quit. Well, don't!

I, too, have an idea of what you are experiencing. At first, it started as a passing thought. I found myself being in the company of people who for years have brought me joy, but I no longer felt jubilant. I was a social, young man in my twenties; I was blessed with a good job that provided financial stability; I had a loving family with strong Christian values, and I was physically healthier than I had ever been. No one who looked at me from the outside would have been able to tell what I was experiencing. Yet, I was plagued with relentless harrowing thoughts that seemed interminable. My unhappiness began to settle in and intensify and no one knew.

I was hesitant to tell anyone because I genuinely was unsure how to begin. As a result, I began to struggle with a whole range of issues. My appetite suffered a substantial reduction. I couldn't recall the last time I enjoyed an activity. Consequently, I began to distance myself from my closest friends without explanation. I continued to tell myself that my experience was simply a season and that with time, I would be fine. This was my experience after years of trying to operate my life at an unsustainable pace. I was living aimlessly and had become utterly overwhelmed.

The good news is that, like mine, your fight is a winnable one. Your opponent thrives on negativity and confusion, and it may seem at times that you've lost. When in reality, the very fact that God has sustained you thus far is a victory. Your antagonist is a conquerable adversary that anyone can defeat throughout their lives.

If you are feeling alone, or afraid, or defeated I want you to know those feelings are temporary. The truth is you're not alone, and you're not a failure. No matter how much you're struggling at work. No matter how few friends you've made recently. No matter the unexpected traumas you've experienced at the expense of close friends and loved ones. The undesirable voice in your head endorsing thoughts like "Will my life ever be normal? I'm probably being punished. Will I ever feel happy again?" That voice is lying to you. You're having these thoughts because you are still trying to grasp the full extent of your battle. Once those feelings are conquered, every aspect of your life will begin to improve. What you are dealing with is not uncommon. In fact, the exact battle you are fighting is more common than you think.

You got your hands on this book because you no longer want to think the way you think. Realizing reclamation is possible is a huge first step. You and I will start to piece together your puzzle to recover your mental wellness and get the most out of your life. I have acquired some essentials from my fight that I'll be sharing with you so that you too can live a more fulfilled life, free of added stresses and strains. To be clear, I am not a clinical psychologist, therapist, or doctor. My unique understanding and skill in this area come from my personal experience reclaiming my own life.

Through my journey, I've learned how important it is to not fight this battle alone. My faith in God has been my timely help every step of the way, and my primary inspiration to write this book. It is my prayer that each chapter will bring you closer to triumph—to a place where you are hopeful, not hopeless; peaceful, not anxious; and free, not overwhelmed.

It is time for you to reclaim your life and through the course of this book, you and I are going to work together to do just that. What you are experiencing is remediable and things can and will improve. What you need are the right mental safeguards and a few guidelines to achieve it. Consider the viewpoints introduced in this book a blueprint; reinforcements to assist in your forthcoming road to triumph.

Smashing the Stigma

Throughout this book, you'll see me refer to mental illness as emotional fragility. I do this to help undo some of the stigma associated with the term *mental illness*, which to me, depicts a concrete diagnosis. I prefer the term emotional fragility which better portrays a rectifiable irregularity.

Our emotions are caused by our thoughts, which we can take steps or get assistance to help protect and strengthen. They are God's way of forewarning us to something we need to pay attention to. They can alert us to what is going on in our hearts, lives, and relationships. Although they can be unpredictable and difficult to describe at times, our emotions are still God's gift to us, and the language of our heart. It's culturally understood that we ought to maintain good physical health to allow our organs to work at their finest. Whereas our mental health is infrequently met with the same level of significance.

For the purpose of this book, you can think of emotional fragility and all associated classifications as soluble challenges we potentially face with anxiety, depression, or addiction. I am not trying to rewrite how the healthcare industry refers to our mental health. Rather, I am challenging you to think about our mental capacity in a slightly different manner where it is crucial for you to have precise discernment in every thought and potential decision that you make.

If you are experiencing suicidal thoughts, please tell someone or seek professional help. You can gain support twenty-four hours/seven days a week by calling your national suicide prevention hotline. Below are the hotlines for the United States, Canada, United Kingdom, Ireland, Australia, and New Zealand.

US: 1-800-273-8255

Canada: 1-833-456-4566

United Kingdom: 0-800-689-5652

Ireland: 353-116-123

Australia: 1300-22-4636

New Zealand: 09-5222-999

1

Unmasking Anxiety

Even though I walk through the darkest valley,
I will fear no evil, for you are with me; your rod and your staff,
they comfort me. – Psalm 23:4

During the weeks leading up to the Covid-19 US government lockdown of 2020, I was amid my evening workout routine. In the middle of a set of abdominal crunches, a sharp pain shot through the left side of my chest. Disturbed, I carefully stood up to relieve the aggrieved area. I stalled, trying to get a sense of what was happening. As I waited, my room began to spin. Putting my hand on a nearby chair, I held on to the backrest to maintain my balance. I pressed my fingers against my chest, trying to locate the throbbing pain, figuring I had only pulled a muscle. I stared at my television, a fixed point, and gazed without blinking until the screen was unrecognizably fuzzy and the pain dissipated. Thankful and relieved, I continued my set.

By my second rep, the pain returned, more persistent and demanding. It was accompanied by a prickling sensation, which started at the fingertips of my left hand and moved up my arm to the shoulder. I took a sip of water and again waited for it to pass. By this time, though, fear had begun to creep in. My heart picked up speed, rocketed forward, and beat boisterously, although this was the standard workout routine that I had completed hundreds of times. Something about seeing my heartbeat protrude through my chest sent me into a panic. My room began spinning, and no position standing or sitting felt cozy enough to settle down. I imagined this type of discomfort is what having a heart attack felt like.

A few of my symptoms would go on for months, and the second I thought I overcame it, it was back. My body was in a full-blown rebellion and had become untrustworthy. I started to question everything, never feeling grounded or safe. I had never experienced issues sleeping at night, but as days turned into weeks, and weeks rolled into months, I became too terrified to rest my eyes. I was trapped inside the walls of my own prison. I knew the sequence and expected it at random times and places. This was the order: my heart would start beating erratically, and then fast and faster. My mouth felt unable to create and sustain saliva followed by difficulty swallowing. And then the stinging sensation, beginning inside of my fingers, sometimes taking a different starting route from my toes. I had it down to a science.

My body was mentally and now physically drained from a lack of sleep, and I had lost my social zeal. Friends reached out to make plans, and I postponed, canceled, or flat out ignored them. The same friends I had once enjoyed being around, I now spurned. For each invitation, I invented the latest reason why I couldn't attend and eventually as I had wished, the requests stopped coming. In part due to the uncertain state of the pandemic, but I assume my endless excuses contributed most.

I've met too many people with similar stories to mine. If you are like many anxiety sufferers, this is likely not your first book or attempt to get answers and help. Regardless of your age, race, religion, or tax bracket, there aren't many physical or emotional feelings more wildly uncomfortable than anxiety. Only past or current sufferers know this for certain. If you are like me, you may have or currently experience one or more of the symptoms I've experienced above, or perhaps some from this list.

- Blurred vision
- Derealization
- Diarrhea
- Dizziness
- Dry mouth
- Fatigue
- Forgetfulness
- Heart palpitations
- Hot flashes or chills
- Insomnia
- Intrusive thoughts
- Loss of appetite
- Migraines
- Muscle tension, tremors, twitching and spasms
- Numb or tingling extremities
- Profuse sweating
- Shortness of breath
- Social Anxiety
- Stomach pain and nausea
- Throat tightness and difficulty swallowing

You might also have experiences or difficulties with anxiety that aren't recognized above. Or you might experience some sporadically. Your hormone levels might be affected. It has amplified your perception and awareness so that you notice physical sensations previously oblivious to you. When combined, these changes have made a lot feel like too much. Fighting anxiety is exhausting, so much so that it is common for sufferers to concurrently experience deep depression.

So, we seek answers. We google and browse. We skim through bookshelves to find the latest quick fix. We seek out therapists, psychologists, and ministers, desperate for answers and relief. The act of searching for a solution is one way to help manage the chaos but being informed is only a fraction of the solution. Before we begin on your road to triumph, it is imperative for you to develop a good working understanding of some common concepts. We will begin by defining fear and anxiety.

FEAR

Fear is an internal alarm that tells us that we are in real or perceived danger. Our fight-or-flight response is hard-wired and predictable. Fear is what helps us quickly press on the brake pedal to avoid hitting a distracted pedestrian on the road. Our body temperature goes up, our reaction time quickens, our breathing and heart rate become faster. We are primed to react in a way that protects our survival. It is our body's built-in mechanism to keep us safe.

ANXIETY

Anxiety by definition is a future-oriented response that we experience without the presence of imminent threat or danger. You may feel that something may go wrong; a strong sense of fear or worry, oftentimes originating from personal experiences and traumatic events. Anxiety also has a learned component. Learning theory suggests that anxiety can be acquired through learning and making associations between certain non-dangerous situations and anxious responses. This means that if we witness another person's response, we may gather that the response is necessary. As a child, if you had an anxious parent or guardian, you may have inherited the predisposition to be anxious, and you may have also learned some responses that triggered concern in the absence of danger. It is common to experience some passing feelings of anxiety. For example, it is normal to feel nervous before an important exam or life-changing job interview. When the anxious temperament becomes chronic, persistent, or disproportionate to the stressor, it becomes an anxiety disorder.

Understanding your triggers allows you to approach your recovery from a place of knowledge rather than fear. Healing requires healthy thinking. Your trial is not your trial. Your trial is the way you think about your trial. Your problem is not your problem; it is the way you look at it. No problem is unsolvable. No life is irredeemable. No one's fate is sealed. No one is unloved or unlovable. The enemy is relentless at attempting to manipulate us into thinking we are. He fills our skies with planes loaded with fear and anxiety, hoping to convince us to allow them to land. The Devil is the master of deceit, but he is not the master of your mind. Best-selling author Max Lucado brilliantly paints a picture in his book *Anxious for Nothing.*

You can be the air traffic controller of your mental airport. You occupy the control tower and can direct the mental traffic of your world. Thoughts circle above, coming and going. If one of them lands, it is because you gave it permission. If it leaves, it is because you directed it to do so. You can select your thought pattern ... Do you want to be happy tomorrow? Then sow seeds of happiness today.

2

War on Worry

Do not be anxious about anything, but in every situation,
by prayer and petition, with thanksgiving,
present your requests to God. – Philippians 4:6

"Why am I here? What is my purpose?" We all have arrived at both questions at some point in our lives. We like to feel like we're consuming earth's resources for a purpose. So, we look to things to define our identities and purposes.

Perhaps the most amazing facts of human life relates to the complexity of our human composition. In his book *God's Rx for Fear and Worry*, Dr. James P. Gills, renowned cataract surgeon, describes the human body in its brilliance, sophistication, and precision:

The heart beats two and a half billion times in an average lifetime and pumps blood over sixty thousand miles of blood vessels. We make two million red blood cells every second. Put side by side, they would circle the Earth at the equator four times. In our lungs at any given moment, we have 150 million air molecules. What the retina of the eye does every one-third of a second would take a supercomputer one hundred years to do. The ear has a million moving parts and in many ways is even more sensitive than the eye. The human brain, at a mere three pounds, is the most complex and orderly arrangement of matter in the universe. The brain can store the equivalent of 4.7 billion books. And it can carry out one thousand trillion logical operations per second.

The marvels of our very creation serve as a catalyst to evoke an appreciation for our lives as they help us understand our finiteness. We grasp our absence of control in the grand scheme of our mortal design and realize the very fact that we exist means that there is a purpose for our lives. So why worry?

Worry hangs over your head like a rain cloud. It alters your very being, emotions, relationships, and work ethic, forcing you to dream small, and as a result, end up living shadows of your life of purpose. The more we worry, the more we'll find to worry about. It is often the root of overthinking.

Life flows from your mind. Truly, where the mind goes, the man follows. Your mind plays a sizable role in the course of your life's journey, crafting most of the circumstances you think about. The enemy knows this and regularly uses your mind to make his starting play, hence the old truism, the mind is the Devil's playground. He has fun tampering with your thoughts, because he knows they are the forerunners to your actions.

Eliminating your fears requires you to identify your triggers. Accept that sometimes you will make mistakes. Just as you cannot control every outcome, understand that every decision may not be correct or best. And that is okay. To err is to be human. The ability to worry isn't a learned behavior; we are born with it. Our sinful nature contributes to feeding us a culture of worry, which we will revisit later. We are bombarded daily with low-spirited rumors from our workplace, friends, and social media accounts. Observe how every news headline that you see evokes an emotional reaction and you'll realize we're constantly given reasons to worry. We don't want to make a habit of allowing meaningless burdens to take residence in our lives, fueling our current qualms.

The constant call to worry leaves you sacrificing your peace. Considering how it preoccupies our minds and debilitates our ability to live in peace, worrying is a real threat to our health. Issues with relationships, jobs, finances, and demands on our time can contribute to serious worry sessions. In excess, anxiety will likely follow. Left uncontrolled anxiety will surely craft depression, emotional anguish, and physical pain. Part of the definition of worry is to be mentally torn apart. Worry tears at any peace of mind we might have. When our peace of mind is disturbed, it produces efforts to combat our initial worry, generating more worry as a result. Worry and fear take root in our lives when our selfish interests blind us from seeing what God wants us to. Certainly, none of us can control the situations and circumstances that can create worry and fear. What we can control is how we respond to adversity, which we are guaranteed to encounter throughout several seasons in our lives.

When we are aligned with God's peace which is based on love rather than fear, it is very difficult to embrace worry. Because God is love, we can trust His power to meet our every need. When we focus on Him, we learn that we do not need to be fearful. God has never promised us life without storms. But He has promised to be there when we face them. As we do our part, He promises to do His. He provides us with an inexplicable calm. We should be worried, but we aren't. We should be upset, but we are comforted. The peace that God gives us amid distress transcends all logic, scheming, and efforts to explain it. "I sought the Lord, and he answered me; he delivered me from all my fears" (Psalm 34:4). Fear and anxiety flourish in comfort. Your trust in God is the greatest remedy against becoming overwhelmed.

Here is how it works. You receive a call from your boss. They would like you to come into their office to discuss some upcoming business changes. You arrive at the intersection of fear and trust.

Fear says…

"I'm in trouble. Why is God allowing this to happen to me? I'm probably being punished for that thing I did."

"It was too good to be true for too long. My streak of good luck is running out. They will probably let me go."

"How will I pay for the new car I just bought? How will I upkeep my rent? I was just starting to do well for myself. I don't know how to break this news to anyone."

Trust says…

"I leave it in God's hands."

Resist the urge to exaggerate, overstate or amplify. Focus on the facts, nothing more. The fact is your boss has summoned you to their office. The news can be either good or bad. Pray, lay claim to every biblical promise you know, and trust that God is in control of whatever news is headed your way.

The scriptures tell us that prayer is the remedy for all of our trials. Whenever we feel anxious or overwhelmed, we should immediately go to God in prayer, boldly and with great sincerity, with both the big and small issues in our lives. Through prayer, we receive God's provision, protection, and peace.

Confident prayer begins with our remembrance of God's magnificence. He promises to give us peace that transcends all understanding that will guard our hearts and minds against all our worries (Philippians 4:7). Go to Him in prayer and with praise. Confess your irrational fears, admit your weaknesses. Then, once God moves, you move too. Listen to Him leading you. He is as near as your next breath.

3

Discernment

The fear of the Lord is the beginning of knowledge,
but fools despise wisdom and instruction. – Proverbs 1:7

In its simplest definition, discernment is nothing more than the ability to judge and perceive things as they are. It is the process of making careful distinctions in our thinking about truth. The ability to think with discernment is synonymous with an ability to think biblically. It is an interior search that seeks to align our own will with the will of God to learn what He is calling us to. No matter how small, every choice we make is an opportunity to align ourselves with His will. Further explained, discernment is a quality of attentiveness to God that, over time, develops into the ability to sense His heart and purpose in any given moment. We become familiar with the tone, quality, and content of His voice. We notice how He is present for us in every situation.

Often, we make choices without taking the time to correctly distinguish the aptness of our decisions. Much more than merely deciding, discerning should be the precondition of decision-making to make good, sound choices.

When it comes to your emotional fragility, it is vital to take the necessary steps to analyze every aspect of your life. There you will be able to locate and acknowledge the source of your fragility. The choices you make, places you visit, or the company you choose to align yourself with. Perhaps unexpected physical or emotional trauma you have experienced or things you've done or said that has caused physical or emotional harm to others. An opportunity shows up to discern for every hand we are dealt.

Discerning and understanding the choices we are met with is crucial because we cannot improve what we don't evaluate. This is true for almost every area of our lives. If a person wants to improve their health condition, they must evaluate medical assistance options. If a person wants to improve their finances, they have to evaluate their means to accumulate additional funds. If a person wants to assess how much value a friend is adding to their life? They must evaluate their relationship with the individual. Suppose a person wants to assess job opportunities. In that case, they must evaluate their skills and what they can potentially contribute to an employer. Evaluation is consequential to the course, direction, and quality of our lives. When our thoughts are carefully assessed before our decisions are made, our choices become easier.

Some decisions can be a bit more cumbersome and complex than some of the aforementioned scenarios. In the case of health conditions, very often, especially in certain areas, it's black and white. The numbers are too high or too low. They should either increase or decrease. But when it comes to certain choices, such as relationships, the emotional attachments we have toward people can often be intoxicating to the degree that impairs our judgment. Intoxication in this sense isn't just limited to alcohol consumption. We can be blindly intoxicated by emotions. It's a reality that must be considered when it comes to decision-making within our relationships.

Decisions are like planes, and every decision has a pilot. Where you end up is determined by who's in the captain's seat. Pausing to evaluate gives us clarity to assess the information we ought to gather and see who and what is controlling our plane. Alternatively, if we don't, we will likely end up making poor, blind decisions with any obstacle we are met with. We end up operating in the dark. If we find ourselves spinning out of control, heading toward a downward trajectory, approaching deep, dark places, it's probably because we have not stilled ourselves to think about what is happening. When an individual is unwilling or unable to adequately assess the path and direction they're going, they will certainly end up crashing. Many relationships crash because those involved aren't sure who is in their cockpit. It is incredibly hard to make good decisions with missing information. Taking a moment to pause allows us to emotionally sober up and allow principle, good judgment, and God's spirit to be the pilot of every decision we make.

There are times when we've had such a long history with people who have made drastic contributions to our lives, that it is difficult to see the relationship as it currently exists. There are also times when we fear the unknown and the uncertainty and discomfort that come with exploring something new. We will often choose comfort over crucial change. But if a person doesn't take the time to discern and ask key and critical questions of themselves about the people in their lives, they won't have the clarity needed to make sound decisions. This is true across all relationship dynamics. It applies to life-long friendships, a marriage, a business partnership, and even family. It is entirely possible to be so comfortable having a close friend around that, for years, you have accepted their toxic behavior as a part of what they contribute to your life. It is possible to be so engaged in being married that once you are wed, you never work on the marriage. It is possible to be so preoccupied with the success of your business that you miss the opportunity to accurately align your ideas with a business partner.

It's also possible to have a family member who may not be supportive and spurn your potential ideas and goals.

And so, assessment in any area is the key to advancement. Discernment helps us to act not just emotionally but intelligently. Relational intelligence is a valuable skill that allows us to appropriately align the individuals that we allow to take residency in our lives.

EVALUATION

Evaluation, as it relates to aligning decisions, is a thinking exercise. Though, to evaluate, we must first ask the right questions. In their "Harvard Business Review", psychologists Susan David and Christina Congleton help us understand how often we subconsciously evaluate:

> Sixteen thousand—that's how many words we speak, on average, each day. So imagine how many unspoken words course through our minds. Most of them are not facts but evaluations and judgments entwined with emotions—some positive and helpful, others negative and less so.

When it comes to evaluating, questioning is one of the key ways we are able to get precise clarity. Right questions give us the right clarity. Good questions give us good clarity. When clarity becomes greater, decisions become easier.

WHERE I AM

Before we can evaluate someone else, it is crucial for us to know what lens we are using. We must ask, "In this season of my life, where am I? Where am I emotionally? Where am I spiritually?" If we cannot locate ourselves, it will be hard to determine where we want a relationship to go. If we don't know where we want to go, we won't know who we're supposed to take with us. Based on your discovery, you will be able to accurately determine what you need.

WHAT I NEED

There are frequent seasons when I need certain things or people in my life who simply are healthy distractions. Of course, that's not all the value they add, but these are the kind of pursuits that allow me to disconnect from a world of work that can be all-consuming. Relationally, the "what do I need?" question requires some thoughtfulness. We have to ask ourselves what it means to have a certain type of person in our lives. People often speak in generalities. We say, "I need good people in my life. I need good friends." The reality of your expectation is that what you need is circumstantial. What is good in one season of your life may not be good in another. Identify what good means to you. Classify what qualities exemplify a good friend and recognize what type of friends will add the most value to you.

WHAT I NEED TO DO

Another question we should propose to ourselves is "what do I need to do?" Do I have to limit my access to someone? Does someone need to be completely disconnected from my life? Does someone else need to be pursued? Although difficult, there will be times when you will have to make beneficial judgments on individuals in your life that will ultimately rework or end your relationships with them. Judgment often carries a negative connotation. The definition at its core is simply "the process of forming an opinion or evaluation by discerning and comparing." If we view judgment as such, then in truth, we're making judgments all the time. We judge whether we like certain foods, clothes, houses, or cars daily.

However, this should not be confused with the religious interpretation. The scriptures tell us that God is able to judge fairly because only He knows everyone's personal circumstance and situation, something we are grossly incapable of.

But we do want to do what the dictionary definition suggests, which is to go through the process of forming an opinion, and then deciding our next steps based on what we discern. You aren't declaring someone good or bad, but simply deciding, based on what you need to do at this juncture in your life, you can no longer accept from them the things you've allowed in the past. The type of judgment necessary in this process is about forming an opinion about whether this individual is good for you now, not whether the individual is good or bad in general.

It is certainly a fine line to walk, considering how easy it is to form assumptions based on people's actions and character. But if we accept the responsibility to determine what is good for our lives, and affirm the goodness of any individual, that distinction will help us recognize the difference. We ultimately must make our own decisions about the role people will play in our lives. Understand where you are. Next, align what you need with what you need to do. The key here is to be brutally honest with yourself to avoid conflicting solutions.

ASSIGNMENTS

There are some scenarios where God will appoint an assignment in the form of an individual in our lives. The assignment might be someone seeking help in an area that you are equipped to aid in. Because we are imperfect, our evaluation of this scenario will sometimes be flawed. Instead of evaluating externally, in this situation, most of our inspections will need to come from within.

What role should I play in this person's life? What qualities do I need to exhibit? What is needed from me in order to fulfill the assignment? All necessary questions we should begin with when faced with this situation. There may be times when we misinterpret how we should work with our assignment, or when we haven't evaluated something as thoroughly as we should have. If we do or say something out of an erroneous evaluation, it is possible to lose our assignment entirely and miss out on an opportunity God has called us to. Hence why discernment before decision-making is so significant. We have to pause and ask the right questions. If the situation allows, take all the time needed to process the information. Most importantly, throughout the entirety of the process, pray for God's guidance to achieve clarity at the crossroads of your decision.

We need to undertake the important task of evaluating our relationships intelligently. We need to recognize the people with whom God has called us to walk in mutually beneficial relationships and to identify those who will derail our destinies or hinder His purposes for our lives. It is important to periodically access our current relationships, and our own behaviors and contribution to these partnerships. As much as we need to assess the people in our lives, we also need to evaluate ourselves to ensure that we aren't becoming the very person we do not want to attract. Our world is full of distractions. It is full of competing voices. It is easy to miss your discernment window by falling victim to other voices that you lose your ability to tell everything else from what God wants you to prioritize.

4

Hold the Line

*Let your conversation be always full of grace, seasoned with salt,
so that you may know how to answer everyone.*
– Colossians 4:6

The quality of our lives is greatly determined by who's in them and how you manage the ones who are a part of it. In other words, the people I allow residency in my life can contribute to my experience of abundant life, or they can contribute to a life of endless agitation. The best relationships are the ones where the people involved want to be. When an individual is an asset in your life and not just a liability. Sometimes we believe this to be true only in the context of marriage or romantic relationships, but it extends so far beyond.

The relationships we have with those we consider friends, people we allow to occupy spaces in our lives, should be covenantal, not transactional. Reciprocity should be distributed equally. When we are in their company, we should be able to say "This is who I am" comfortably without wavering. This does not mean we don't grow or evolve, but those relationships should allow us to be our authentic selves throughout our progression.

Unfortunately, our emotional attachment to others will often blind us to the reality of where they are in life and whether it's safe for us to be in a relationship with them. That coworker who frowns at your employee recognition. That long-time classmate who doesn't want you to befriend anyone else. That family member who makes a point to shame you at the family gathering. These people are likely not your friends, despite the proximity or length of time you've known them.

When it comes to families, this pill is even more difficult to swallow. We expect those we've known for a large part of our lives to be loving, supportive, and honorable. However, there are times when those who claim to have your best interest, say and do more harm to you than maybe a stranger might. As hard as these things can be to believe, we must accept them. The emotional attachment and familiarity one grows accustomed to in a relationship are very real, and it can be incredibly difficult to accept what we see. If we assume that everyone in our lives is supposed to remain a part of our lives, we likely have a grossly unrealistic view of relationships. There will certainly be times when a relationship must come to an end.

TOXIC RELATIONSHIPS

If someone is getting in the way of becoming the person God has created you to be, or frustrating the work He has called you to do, for you that person is toxic. Toxic individuals aren't just difficult people. They may not even be troublesome people. In fact, it is not uncommon for these individuals to display pleasant qualities in some areas. However, for the life of purpose you want, they are simply unfit. It is easy to be blinded by this fact and end up allowing unhealthiness to linger in our lives longer than it should. These cunning individuals are masters at invoking guilt and discouragement.

The challenge is that there is no one exhaustive definition of a toxic person. Toxic has a special designation that we can learn to discern and then manage accordingly. Certain traits are common: They are often draining instead of supportive, and they are users instead of aiders. They can seemingly come across as addicted to self-righteousness, rash judgments and thus frequently disagreeing with others. They may be covertly jealous of peaceful people, families, and friendships and spend much of their time and effort trying to bring others down to their level of misery. They often seek control over your life and at times, it may feel as if they just want you to stop being you. They can be master manipulators: many of them know just how much is "too much" and will control their toxicity so that you will remain in their lives. You may even begin to blame yourself for their behavior. They can be great actors, showing one face to you and another to the rest of the world. To summarize, toxic people rob us of our genuine joy and peace and can often make us question our sanity.

It's time to call them out. It's time for you to take complete control of your life, and that means you will have to learn to play a little defense. Resolve today the certain toxic person that in the past you've allowed to stick around, will no longer be a distraction to you. The sooner we identify these unfit individuals, the sooner we can act to limit or completely disconnect the access that they have to us.

BOUNDARIES / LIMITATIONS

Most of us are aware that limits and structure in every aspect of our lives are good to have, although it isn't uncommon to find individuals that struggle to maintain consistency honoring self-imposed parameters. If you were fortunate, you had a parent or guardian who modeled healthy habits and made sure you did things like brush your teeth and go to bed on time, in a way you could understand, and explained the repercussions if you didn't. Over time, you internalized those basic boundaries and now set them for yourself. You learned that boundaries make life more predictable, which makes you feel more in control in the driver's seat. You learned how to make healthy choices and the consequential importance of self-care. We thrive when our goals and responsibilities are well-defined, when our yes means yes and our no means no.

Unfortunately, there are many cases where these types of boundaries are not taught from a young age. It makes sense that you might struggle to set them for yourself now. Being able to stay up as late as you want, drinking as much soda as you want, and having company over a certain time is fun when you're ten years old. As you grow older, you start to realize the severe health and relational implications you can begin to experience as a result.

Setting a boundary can be a proactive or preemptive decision. You may decide it is best to not give someone complete access to yourself in the first place. Or we may at times find ourselves in situations where people simply won't adhere to giving us the space we have requested. Therefore, an integral part of being a responsible adult is setting boundaries for ourselves. Boundaries are personal guidelines. They are limitations we set regarding what we will permit or allow. We need limits to keep ourselves physically, mentally, spiritually, and emotionally healthy—making choices that are in our own best interest even when they aren't enjoyable in the moment. Boundaries help you monitor your own behavior and create a healthy structure for your life. When you set a boundary for yourself, you're saying: "Here's the line between what's okay for me at this moment in time and what isn't. Here's the line that I won't cross or allow someone else to cross under any circumstances." Clear boundaries communicate who we are and are fully dependent on the life of purpose we want.

To be clear, the purpose of boundaries isn't necessarily to control what someone else does, but rather to protect us from their negative traits. One of the greatest mistakes people make with attempting to patch friendships is communicating to others what they need to do to make the boundary work. Our restrictions won't stop them from being who they are. Boundaries won't make an untrustworthy person honest. They won't make a compulsive person more disciplined. The nature of the boundary unfortunately won't change how they act, but what it will do is reveal to you the nature of the friendship.

Set a boundary to ensure you will never tell an untrustworthy person any intimate secrets. Set another to make sure that you won't take a dishonest person at their word. Set one to let a dominative person know that decisions regarding your life will no longer be collaborative. In situations where the time invested with this person is already limited, boundaries become a bit easier to set. It can become much more challenging with closer proximity and engagement to an individual. In this case, a conversation centered around your decision likely will have to be had. Remember, it is essential to recognize that you are only responsible for your own thoughts and behaviors. You cannot control how the other person reacts.

It's counterproductive and unrealistic to expect perfection all the time. When you struggle with a boundary, identify your mistake and reaffirm it. Explore the reasons for slipping up, adjust your boundaries, if needed, and make a plan to improve. You're going to need God's guidance and strength as you venture out into this new territory. Sit with Him until you have finished emptying yourself of the thoughts and feelings that you've been struggling with. Then, when you have found comfort and security in your decision, pray for God's guidance. He created you to be unique. This is important because you will not be able to set clear boundaries until you are clear on your desires. Pray unceasingly for the things you want, while you work diligently for the things you need.

CONVERSATIONS

It is unnecessary to announce every relational adjustment that you make. There will be times when you can make adjustments without communicating them. An announcement may not be required for a relationship with limited engagement. However, there are situations where we must engage in some type of conversation. If you refuse to, your target may notice the shift and inquire about your unannounced change in behavior. Be ready to have an honest, direct approach to avoid no room for misinterpretation. The focus should remain that the change being made is necessary for what you need at this moment and not necessarily what they are able or unable to offer.

A way to begin this conversation may look like this: "In the past, for whatever reason, I've allowed more unhappiness than I should have. For my own emotional wellness, I will be focusing more on myself going forward. I need to feel comfortable while this is taking place and will be making some adjustments in our relationship for my peace of mind." Notice the framing of this still focuses on your needs in setting the limit. It isn't condescending or accusatory, but it still addresses the issue and sets the precedent of your boundary.

For every variation of these conversations, there is a degree of courage that you will need to obtain. It takes a certain valor to make abrupt, necessary changes in your relationships. In addition to courage, sincerity will have to drive these conversations. We must understand that being authentic will allow us to walk away freely without regret. Not being candid will likely exacerbate the damage both parties will experience later on.

You likely will receive a negative response to your conversation. Oftentimes, we may delay having these essential conversations due to fear of causing or feeling pain. You might even be inclined to change your mind. We should never allow fear the opportunity to handicap our decision-making. It can be difficult to remain steadfast in the face of disruption in a relationship. But a big part of how we deal with the repercussions of a tough conversation has to do with how we prepare ourselves before. We must consider how to brace ourselves for the potential reactions from the individual.

When it comes to preparation, we will never be able to predict how we will feel during the conversation. However, what we can do is prepare ourselves for how we are going to react. Consider how you might respond to each potential reaction. Examining these different scenarios ahead of time will allow time to discover the best approach and overcome any backpedaling we may be inclined to do.

These conversations are not only good for the relationships that we no longer want or need, but they are equally good for us. They expose areas of our own lives that we may need to focus on. In fact, these conversations will help to facilitate our personal growth. Don't delay the inevitable. Putting off the "limitation" conversations we need to have with people in our lives only hurts more in the long run.

ACCEPTING THE REALITY

The first step to letting go of unwanted individuals is to accept the reality of the situation. You will have to ask yourself, "Does this particular person in my life bring me joy?" If the answer is not overwhelmingly yes, you will have to accept that fact. People do change, unfortunately, this type of person rarely does enough to stick around and wait. You will have to come to terms that this is who they are. In frequent cases, a person may portray undesirable qualities much later on. Relationships are not always static, but fluid. We must be able to recognize and discern when something is shifting.

LETTING GO

Once we have accepted the reality of the situation, and our boundaries have not provided the solutions we had hoped for, we must now move on to the decision to let go of the person indefinitely. Often, we hold on to unhealthy people and situations because we are afraid of being perceived as impolite. Also, there are times when we don't want to remove someone because we recognize that this person contributes more to our life than solely negativity. Maybe there's some value this person adds that makes eliminating them difficult. You may find yourself reasoning internally by saying things like, "It's not all bad." or "I don't want to give up on them yet." Both of which are plausible thoughts.

This is something that I have struggled with habitually in the past. For years, I struggled with the idea of making necessary eliminations. I felt as though God has been so incredibly patient with me time and time again, that I owed the same level of patience to others. Unfortunately, I allowed some individuals to linger much longer than they should have. At times, it felt like I was living several different lives to please different people. Not because I enjoyed it, but I sincerely felt that these certain individuals needed me in their lives for one reason or another. I failed to see elimination as an opportunity for both parties to pursue what God had in store next.

This can be the reality in all types of relationships. When a romantic relationship isn't working out, ending it is a gift you give to both parties involved. The same goes for a family member or coworker relationship. We should rethink letting go of others as releasing them to pursue God's next and best. No matter how much it hurts to let people go, the damage is far greater to let them stay. When boundaries have not worked and it is clear that the relationship is working in direct opposition to what you would like God to do in your life, it is time to consider letting go.

God has woven His purposes into every one of our experiences—even the difficult ones. As we voyage to discover the meaning God has infused into our lives and relationships, we will find the strength necessary to make positive changes.

5

Smoke and Mirrors

For our struggle is not against flesh and blood,
but against the rulers, against the authorities,
against the powers of this dark world and against the spiritual
forces of evil in the heavenly realms. – Ephesians 6:12

Sometimes you don't feel in absolute control. But when you seek help from others, including a medical clinician or specialist, rarely do you find precise answers. Instead, you're met with disapproval from doctors who might be inclined to generalize your experience. Conventional medical treatment options often feel more like judgment than help. Doctors are taught to focus on physical symptoms. Can't sleep? There's a pill for that. Depressed? Here's some medication. Overcome with anxiety? There are pills for that too. Side effects from all those meds you're on? There are pills for those as well!

Just as every human fingerprint is unique, every person's brain offers a unique challenge, and thus requires a unique approach to identify and unscramble what you are suffering. In this chapter, we will tackle the subtle topic of addiction.

CREATURES OF HABIT?

Cravings aren't static. You can go weeks, months, or even years without your fix, but then relapse again, going from mild to severe in a matter of seconds. The truth is that each person's struggle with fixation is unique. At the same time, it isn't a weak individual that yields to the pressure, just as it isn't a weak individual that succumbs to cancer, or any other health irregularities. In part, it is our genetic vulnerabilities along with environmental toxins and influences that create the fertile ground within which addictions develop.

Addiction is far more complicated than just saying "No". It's when your repetitive use, or behavior—and your extreme preoccupation with it—gets beyond your control. You can't stop even if you want to. When you attempt to quit, you experience overwhelming cravings and severe withdrawal symptoms. You need more and more to get the same effects. Your only relief from withdrawal comes from indulging again. Every cell in your body tells you, "I need this." You suspect or even know that you're in trouble, but you ignore the warning signs. We are overly familiar with common vices such as alcohol and drugs. Often, we fail to realize that certain activities—such as gambling, compulsive shopping, and sex addictions including indulging in pornography, to name a few can be highly addictive.

Our obsessions might begin as a way for us to mask our pain. Someone might be attracted to drinking or smoking because they are seeking relief—from a painful past, from anxiety, from thoughts and feelings that they are not sure how to deal with. If left unsettled, the band-aids we apply to our underlying issues become more and more difficult to heal. In this chapter, we will uncover the blueprint you'll need to find freedom from compulsive behaviors and withdrawal symptoms.

Let's deal with a few common vices.

SEX

Normal people think about sex, and to fanatisize infrequently is to be human. Sex addicts, however, think about sex almost endlessly. While many people might note an attractive person then move on with their activities, sex addicts do not. Instead, they wonder how they might obtain sex with that person, or they envisage what sex with that person would be like. This sensual mentality is an unfortunate product of the tools at our disposal. The accessibility, affordability, and anonymity of the internet make for an unwavering foundation. These days, it is difficult to find a popular television show on Netflix or other streaming platforms, without a heavy dose of physical or implied sexual activity.

We should also consider that we live in a time in which the use of pornography is increasing dramatically. Our cultural appetite for carnal content has heightened in addictive ways and we are paying the price for it. Most of us would probably agree that pornography is displaying or writing about in some medium, nudity or sexual activity that incites sensual feelings.

Pornography shouldn't just be defined as just that. If that were the case, many works in art exhibits would be considered pornographic. Furthermore, there are instances of pornography on television that display no nudity at all. For example, many television shows and movies don't show explicit nudity (although some come close) but do portray sexually suggestive or explicit sexual situations. Could this not also be considered pornographic?

It is important to note that a sex addict doesn't have to be someone who craves all kinds of visual or written stimuli. Additionally, the definition of sexual addiction does not depend on the number of partners or even the frequency of relations. But rather on why addicts practice what they do and whether they can break the behavior. Therefore, it is plausible for a person with one sexual partner to be addicted to sex if it is used to escape undesirable feelings, rather than express intimacy between themselves and a significant other.

ALCOHOL

You or the person that comes to mind when reading this passage may not want to be identified as an alcoholic. But here's what everyone with a drinking problem has in common. At some point you crossed a line. You went too far. Maybe you blacked out. Maybe you drove while intoxicated. Maybe you destroyed a relationship with alcohol-fueled verbal or physical abuse. Regardless of your specific circumstance, you reached a point where you felt out of control. One drink triggered an irresistible, unstoppable, all-consuming craving for more. Then you started hating yourself for it. Ashamed, remorseful, and miserable, you inevitably drank again. As with all addictions, what may have started out as a sporadic, socially accepted, and even a doctor-approved drink or two, quickly became an everyday occurrence, increasing in frequency and quantity.

Western culture has the largest role to play on how alcohol is perceived by the masses. Despite the grim statistics, Americans embrace and encourage drinking far more than they do other vices. It is the one item almost universally accepted at social gatherings that routinely causes regret. Sure, it is fine if you want to cut back on drinking for personal reasons, and people are happy to tell you not to drink and drive. However, warning others about binge drinking will win you few friends.

Of course, many people have a normal relationship with alcohol, which has been a fixture of social life since the time of the Sumerians and ancient Egyptians. But today, what actually constitutes a "normal" relationship with alcohol can be difficult to determine, because American views have been influenced by decades of careful marketing and lobbying efforts. Specifically, beer, wine, and spirit manufacturers have repeatedly tried to normalize and exculpate binge drinking. The alcohol industry has done a great job of marketing the product and using its influence to frame the idea that hazardous drinking is the problem, and as long as you drink safely, you're fine. Which in theory is correct, although for addicts, habitually unrealistic.

Alcoholism can be a long, painful, and slow suicide punctuated, perhaps, by good times and good feelings. At some point, most heavy drinkers realize they are killing themselves. Damage to the liver, which is responsible for purging the very same undesirable toxic chemicals drinkers ingest, gastrointestinal issues, and considerable reduction of brain and muscle function are not uncommon.

I am not by any means saying it is never okay to have a drink, as conversely, there have been proven health benefits when consumed in moderation. Drinking red wine a few times a week has been associated with reduced risk of heart disease. Drinking alcohol in moderation has also been associated with longevity. However, with anything we do, self-control should be exhibited, and drinking is no different. Know your limit and own it.

Recovering from alcoholism is about your willingness to be honest with yourself and others, to work as hard as you can to change, to understand that you may fall on your face many times, to learn to ask for and receive help, and ultimately to find a way to love yourself enough that you commit to no longer harming yourself.

DIGITAL MEDIA

There's so much good that comes from having technology at our fingertips. Easy access to friends, instant walking or driving directions, a weather report no farther away than your back pocket, to say nothing of the ability to dictate or jot down notes the minute you think of something important. For those of us who are easily distracted and don't do well sitting quietly for more than a minute or two, a smartphone is a lifesaver. Our little screens allow us to complete so much.

To have so much information, and activities available to you at the touch of a button is exciting. And doing a little online shopping, getting lost in time scrolling through Tiktok, or sharing your latest thoughts on Twitter is a satisfying way to unwind at the end of a stressful day. The digital world is an integral part of modern-day life for the vast majority of Americans. We spend a lot of time on devices both creating and consuming (but mostly consuming) digital media. But for all the opportunities created, unfortunately using this much has repercussions for both your mental and physical health.

Even if your mind doesn't spin in several directions at once as mine often does, the endless access to information and digital technology is likely fragmenting your attention. You may suspect you are spending too much time on screens. If you have struggled with digital media, in particular social media, chances are you probably already know you have a problem.

Every time you receive a social media notification, your brain feels a rush of pleasure, a hit of dopamine. Dopamine is the chemical messenger that is released in your brain when you anticipate or receive something positive or pleasurable. It signals the brain to pay attention. Its message is that whatever is about to be experienced—a delicious scent, eye contact with an individual that you deem attractive, a glass of wine, is worthwhile. Screens are so enticing to the brain that Peter C. Whybrow, director of UCLA's Semel Institute for Neuroscience and Human Behavior, calls them "electronic cocaine."

When you acknowledge the distraction, gauge your ability to get off your phone screen for consecutive hours. Scheduling a walk or run or trip to the gym, where you leave the phone behind, is a good way to begin. Next, try cleansing your phone from all social media apps for extended periods. Try to keep your calendar as busy as possible to avoid a relapse.

Until very recently, we all lived just fine without twenty-four/seven access to Tiktok, Twitter, and Instagram. Although complete abstinence from screens would be as unrealistic as complete abstinence from eating daily, you can place your screen use into proper perspective by remembering what matters most to you and filling your life with activities that free you from your smart devices.

SPIRITUAL INFLUENCES

The concept of addiction clarifies and deepens our understanding of the consequences of sin. In the same breath that most acknowledge the existence of good and bad, light and dark, heaven and hell, and the notion that certain guardian angels are elected to protect us, we ought to know from whom or what. In accepting your addiction as a sin, we must also accept that the Devil, the personification of evil, is at work. As the scriptures tell us, Satan comes only to steal and kill and destroy (John 10:10). He uses many strategies to create potential addictions, including environmental influences, unhealthy family dynamics, and abuse. The enemy convinces us that we are immoral and irredeemable. He sows hopelessness by convincing us that we won't get well. There is no doubt that we engage in intense spiritual warfare whenever we attempt to heal our personal compulsions, which we will further examine in the next chapter.

Whatever your individual battle, the key is whether you really want to change. Vibrant health requires embracing a new lifestyle. If there is any reluctance in your decision, no strategy, however simple, will work. Can one really trust God to eliminate your addiction? As someone that has overcome the obsessions listed above, the answer is unequivocally "Yes!" I will admit, though, pride is a challenging obstacle to overcome. The sin of pride is at the heart of this challenge and anyone who wants to heal must first get past the hurts and anger of the past in order to say yes to God. It all starts with forgiveness.

Only in a relationship with God do we satisfy our deep spiritual and emotional thirst. All the false substitutes and idolatries of our world can never satisfy us the way He can. In order to heal, addicts must begin to acknowledge that all of their other efforts to satisfy their thirsts are abysmal failures.

Imagine a person who is dying of thirst. Now consider God's love as living water which gives us life. Many people want to experience living water, the grace of God's forgiveness. Their minds, however, are like old coffee filters, cluttered with grime. If the wounds of our past have dumped shameful messages into our emotional filters, anything we pour through those filters comes out looking and feeling like shame. Even the living water of God's love for us comes out as shame because we don't believe we are deserving of it. We must begin to put new messages into our filters to truly embrace what God promises to us. Although we can never eliminate the old messages from our memories, we can slowly diminish their power by reminding ourselves daily of the truth about God's love. Acquiring this mindset, we will quench our thirst.

6

Falsities and Fabrications

*Dear friends, do not believe every spirit,
but test the spirits to see whether they are from God,
because many false prophets have gone out into the world.*
— 1 John 4:1

The Bible teaches that there is a seen physical world and an unseen spiritual world—both worlds are created by God—surrounding us whether we understand it or not. If this is so, how much notice should we take of the unseen world? It seems that interest in the supernatural is greater than ever. Unwittingly, there is a real battle of good against evil taking place in our world and in our individual lives.

What about tarot cards and fortune-telling? Where is the harm in horoscopes? And ghost-hunters, who for a price will rid your home of ghosts? After all, not many people seriously believe in the Devil and what he's capable of, do they? Be warned, he is real, as the Bible teaches throughout the Old and New Testaments, and he is most definitely believed to be real by Jesus. Christ warned of false messiahs and false prophets who would be a menace to the faith of his believers (See Matthew 24:23-24). Although Satan is not mentioned here by name, it is clear from the epistles that he is in fact the propagator of these attractive anti-Christian ideas. He has his ministers who pose as being on the side of righteousness

(See 2 Corinthians 11:13-15) as he makes them appear to be inspired prophets.

It is important for us to explore what occurs in the spiritual world and focus on the difference between using our untapped abilities for good and being deceived by the enemy into misusing them.

Psychics, séances, tarot card readers, and mediums are increasingly considered normal. Practitioners may use varied methods ranging from cards, tea leaves, and crystal balls to determine the future of their consumers. Whatever the method, probably some degree of clairvoyance is involved. Despite it gaining rapid traction and popularity, in Deuteronomy 18:10-11, God specifically forbids fortune-telling. The realm of future events, like the realm of the return of the spirits after death, belongs to God. However, God discloses certain future crises in the Bible, and from time to time I do believe He shows us or grants us an intuition of some coming event in our own lives. This may simply come to us through some dream, experience, or situation, and become meaningful when we later encounter the someone or thing for which God was preparing us. Note, this is different from our deliberate peering into the future.

Now if we accept the fact that Satan is primarily concerned to divert us into alternatives to the gospel, then we must be prepared for him to offer these alternatives in the form of plausible psychic and spiritual experiences. We then assume a realm and activities whereby, without introducing the intervention of spirit beings, some people can project an invisible influence beyond the reach of their physical senses.

CONSULTING THE CARDS

Knowledge of the future tends to nurture a passive attitude toward life. We would quickly become optimistic or pessimistic in light of what we discovered about our future. An impending fortune makes us careless with money today; the threat of an accident keeps us on edge for weeks. The book of Ecclesiastes, among its many wise thoughts, teaches that men and women must face an unseen future by trusting God who alone knows everything.

Some people refuse to make any important decision without consulting the tarot cards. Either by their acquired inner resources or by collusion with spirit entities or both, the practitioner attains mysterious power that is not open to the average person.

God does not intend for us to have absolute certainty about the future, but lacking foreknowledge, to use our common sense. When we ask for God's guidance, this must take account of our being in an uncertain world situation; God will not necessarily alter the situation to suit our convenience either. Still, it is important to note that habitual dependence on these fortune-tellers will ultimately decrease trust in God. The fortune-teller puts himself into a semi-divine position, giving their patrons the impression that they can turn to them to discover what God would otherwise conceal from them.

CHANNELING ASTROLOGY

Astrology began when people started to look for meanings in some of the movements of the planets against the fixed pattern of the stars. During this time, the signs were applied to national events rather than to individuals. This is how the prophet Isaiah viewed astrology when he foretold the doom of Babylon. "Let your astrologers come forward, those stargazers who make predictions month by month, let them save you from what is coming upon you" (Isaiah 47:13). It is uncertain when individual horoscopes based on birthdates began. Likely, it originated as advice about good or bad days for an individual to take some important step. In Imperial Rome deductions were drawn from the sign of the Zodiac under which a person was born, and the emperors Augustus, Tiberius, Caligula, and Claudius all had court astrologers to advise them concerning the position of the planets in relation to their sun sign. Probably, their advice was much the same as is found in common horoscope applications today. Astrologers gradually moved toward more detailed horoscopes where until today it is regarded as essential to know the exact date of birth.

Astrologers are divided in their emphases on whether the planets, sun, and moon actually affect a person's life, or whether their positions merely indicate the internal and external influences that a person is encountering from birth and at a particular moment. The former view began with the linking of the planets with powerful gods and goddesses. This underlies the warning the Bible gives us not to worship the host of heaven and treat them as gods. "And when you look up to the sky and see the sun, the moon, and the stars—all the heavenly array—do not be enticed into bowing down to them and worshiping things the Lord your God has apportioned to all the nations under heaven" (Deuteronomy 4:19).

Thus, as a Christian, it is difficult for me to believe that our lives are governed by the position of the planets or the phases of the moon. This would be a direct insult to who God is. In the same breath, we ought not to revere horoscopes as all-knowing, as we would be guilty of openly denouncing the very first and arguably, most significant commandment. "You shall have no other gods before me" (Exodus 20:3).

Personally, I advise against seeking out an astrologer to have a reading of your progressed horoscope which claims to show how you are being influenced now and in the future. The interpretation may be correct, and I have no doubt that forecasts may be given by clairvoyance, the horoscope providing a connection with the persons themselves. But I must stress that I do not believe God means for us to guide our lives by the predictions of horoscopes, crystal balls, or other similar classifications.

YOGA OR FITNESS?

Ever thought about whether Half Moon, Figure Four, and High Dragon were consistent with your faith? Or even had anything to do with it at all? Yoga has many contexts, many types of instructors, and people who practice it for all different reasons. It is widely considered one of the better ways to improve both physical and mental well-being, where the number of people turning to yoga for bettering the quality of their lives is growing regularly.

Most closely associated with Eastern religions like Hinduism and Buddhism, many who practice yoga use it with meditation and as part of achieving the spiritual goals of unity with God and nature as well as unity with what is called your "divine self." The concern for Christians is, the Bible tells us to meditate on God's Word, that we are not divine in ourselves, and that God and nature are not equal. The religious teachings embraced by these belief systems are in conflict with the teachings of Jesus and the writings of the Bible. Christianity is unable to accept the idea that God and nature could be one. There is a Creator and His creation. The creation is not to be worshipped or revered. It is also taught that the physical body is a temple for the Holy Spirit, who is divine, but humans do not possess their own divinity without Him. Therefore, the idea that an extra level of enlightenment is needed to be united to God does not match. We are one with Him because of the presence of His Spirit in us at the point we come to truly believe in the saving power of the death and resurrection of Jesus.

As He promises us free will, God gives grace and wisdom to people who will never know, love, or follow Him. His knowledge and aid are everywhere in our world for us to discover and use to live well. The knowledge of muscle-stretching and overall health benefits from yoga movements is no different. Contorting our bodies into strenuous positions does not mean we subscribe to an entire belief system. However, any yoga practice might be a bad idea if you aren't standing on a strong foundation of good teaching in your faith. It can be confusing as there are many appealing spiritual ideas presented in most practices. It would be easy to accidentally accept conflicting beliefs and philosophies to your faith without even knowing it. Good counsel, discernment, and a pretty clear understanding of what you believe in should be considered. There are plenty of people who practice physical yoga poses strictly for bodily benefits. Before your next hot yoga class, draw some lines. Be someone who discerns even everyday activities like attending a yoga class. Don't stop short of thinking through the implications of what yoga means to you and what you're actually doing when you practice it.

Similarly, we need not be dubious of meditation if properly directed. In fact, Christian meditation is anchored to what God has revealed in Scripture. Meditation should, for example, be on Christ as the Bread of life, or the Way; or it might soak in a verse from the daily Scripture portion in the Bible app. Generally, we relate our meditation to union with God. Its misuse is what allows the mind to go passive and accept whatever comes up from the depths, as with an LSD trip.

When all is said and done, it isn't the smartest decision to have contact with the spirit world other than with God. The hunger of the heart is meant to find satisfaction in God, but it is possible to pull aside the blanket of the dark and stumble upon unsolicited forces and experiences. One may even break into a world of entities that are enticing without making demands for moral and spiritual obedience. If contacts were impossible, God would hardly have banned them. In our free-thinking society, there are certain activities in which people indulge simply because they are available. They are not, for this reason, advisable or right. Drugs may break through the barrier of consciousness, but they damage the personality. Smoking eases tension but does more bodily harm than good. So, God who knows all, warns against satisfying our curiosity by consulting spirits or looking to His creations for answers.

7

Strength in Numbers

Two are better than one, because they have a good return for their labor: If either of them falls down, one can help the other up. But pity anyone who falls and has no one to help them up.
— Ecclesiastes 4:9-10

Cindy, twenty-three, a singer and dancer on YouTube, had more than ten thousand subscribers. She had recently overcome severe anxiety and depression two years prior, when a woman she knew since childhood, began tormenting her at her workplace. Cindy had been putting up with the workplace harassment for over a year, which matured into online slandering, loss of friends, and subscribers alike. The harassment became so cruel, that people would come to the door of her home and vandalize her property. She began to receive numerous death threats from ex-fans, and coworkers. She sent money to her tormentor in a desperate hope that the pestering would stop. A few years ago, I witnessed Cindy jump from an eighteen-story hotel rooftop to her death.

Friendship is truly a luxury. Consider your current friend(s) for a moment. It is likely that your shared common interests determine what you talk about and what you do together as friends. These common interests become integral to close friendships because, without them, you would have little to keep the relationship afloat. If your friend is happy, you'll likely enjoy the sentiment. If he or she is agitated, you'll feel this too. This is why it's said that you are who your friends are. In other words, you take on the qualities and characteristics of those friends with whom you choose to spend your time. This permits the opening to consult about situations in your life with certainty they will relate.

You might have also experienced what it is like to not have an outlet, where you don't share insecurities with the people in your life. You are unsure of when and how to begin. Or perhaps, you have a friend in mind but at times, you are hesitant to share because you are beginning to feel like a burden. Learning of Cindy's unfortunate decision, we recognize the significance of having that person.

There are many aspects of myself that allow me to connect with one friend, but not necessarily the same aspects that permit me to connect with another friend. There may be some overlap between these characteristics so that one friend might share a lot in common with another. Because no single person aligns perfectly with everything about me, it isn't the best idea to expect one person to be my only friend. Also, it isn't fair to expect a photocopy of yourself in a friend, as no one person perfectly shares all your ambitions.

Hence, several friends provide different things. The range and kind of friends that you select will be unique to what you need, expect, and are willing to give. Reciprocity is at the heart of friendship. This reciprocity is always of an inexact, probably immeasurable, doubtless best left unmeasured, nature. To ask for pure equivalence from a friend—I did this for you, therefore you must perform an act of precisely equal significance for me—is impossible and should never be required. Further, before you allow an individual into your space, see that your decision is unhurried and carefully considered. Revisit Chapter 3 as it will better guide your assessment.

HELPING A FRIEND

There are many ways to make a difference in another person's life. And not one of them takes very much effort or planning. These guidelines are not based so much on what I've gained from researching, but what I've learned from my own experience, having dealt with emotional fragility myself and then possessing a leadership role where I am regularly consulted by others. The help that you are able to provide is in part determined by your relationship with them. A depressed person is unlikely to share and talk about what they're experiencing. They are more likely to avoid conversation and the opportunity to share their grievances.

Knowing this, you can assure them that you care. One of the greatest fears a depressed individual has is rejection by others. A quick text or call saying, "You've been on my mind" or "I am praying for you" is no small gesture. Even when we don't feel like praying, if we keep our minds quiet and our hearts open, we will become aware of God's presence and will be guided to do the next right thing on behalf of whoever is in our focus. We don't have to do a lot of work to make a positive difference in the lives of the people who are sharing our journey.

Further, advise the person to seek professional help from a competent counselor. This can come in the form of a psychiatrist, psychologist, spiritual leader, or advisor. Frequently, a professionally trained counselor is necessary to provide timely assistance in certain areas. Encourage your helpee to seek professional attention as anxiety and depression can sometimes be aggravated by certain medical conditions that need to be addressed. Additionally, do not discount the ability of religious members who have experienced similar obstacles to providing invaluable insight and aid. In addition to the mental and emotional burden, depression and anxiety taps into a spiritual element that should be addressed pastorally from the scriptures.

Remember, either from your own experience or that of others, an emotionally fragile person likely will be reluctant to seek help on their own. The initiative will not always be there, and you will have to help the said person find the drive or potentially accompany them to seek a professional. Be aware to always get consent when attempting to assist. It is critical to not break trust during this process which is certain to occur if boundaries are overstepped. Trust between you and this person is the foundation of your ability to support them. It is important that you are available to provide emotional or spiritual help. The role that you assume here will often be a secondary one in support of professionals that are providing primary care, but also important.

Although the person you would like to help might be someone you love dearly, it is a real danger that soon, your entire life becomes helping your loved one overcome their battle. Understand you don't have it in your power to conquer someone else's fight. That decision is ultimately up to the individual. Support, but draw boundaries so that their experience doesn't consume your life. The help you contribute should rather strengthen you to support another individual should another opportunity present itself.

8

Faith Over Fear

For we live by faith, not by sight. – 2 Corinthians 5:7

STRENGTH THROUGH THE STRUGGLE

The wind rushed through Aubrey's jet-black hair as the eleven-year-old boy made his way through the familiar streets from school to his home. Just a couple of blocks from home, Aubrey found the cocoon of a butterfly. He stared at it for several minutes and made note of where it was so he could keep an eye on it during the next few days.

The following week, he noticed a small opening in the cocoon. Aubrey lost complete track of time as he sat and watched the insect inside struggle to force its body through the tiny hole. As the sun began to set, he hurried home but couldn't stop thinking about the cocoon. The next day, after school, Aubrey noticed the insect appeared as though it had gotten as far as it could and helplessly remained mostly inside the cocoon.

The next morning, he took a pair of scissors and put them in his backpack. On the way to school, he stopped again to look at the cocoon. Feeling sorry for the insect, he decided to help it enter the outside world. He carefully snipped off the remaining bit of the cocoon foundation. Aubrey smiled as he watched the butterfly emerge smoothly from the hole. He was surprised to notice the butterfly's swollen body and small shriveled wings.

Aubrey continued to observe the butterfly because in his child-like innocence he expected at any moment its wings would enlarge and expand to be able to support its body.

That didn't happen. In fact, the butterfly spent the rest of its life crawling around with a swollen body and shriveled wings. It was never able to fly. What Aubrey didn't understand was that the restricting cocoon and the struggle required for the butterfly to get through the tiny opening were God's way of forcing fluid into its wings so that it would be ready for flight. Sometimes struggles are exactly what we need in our lives. Though none of us enjoy them, God uses them for our benefit. He increases our faith when we call on Him for help and strengthens us during our darkest hours.

If God allowed us to go through our lives obstacle-free, it would cripple us. We wouldn't be as strong as we are. We would never fly. Trust Him wholeheartedly through your shaky wings and daily struggles. Instead of growing frustrated with all that is going wrong in your life, try shifting your focus to what you will become after the struggles cease. Find complete solace in the fact that God's timing is always the right timing.

Growing your confidence in walking by faith isn't easy. Consider this rebellion taken from the Bible that erupted within the Children of Israel on their exodus from Egypt. After the Lord had given His people manna (bread from heaven) to eat, some complainers amongst them grumbled that in Egypt they were able to maintain a well-rounded diet. Interestingly, in Egypt, they had earlier cried to God to free them from their enslavers, from which I infer that as slaves they may not have truthfully had such a varied diet. It is easy to dwell on the misfortune of our current situation. During stormy times we can easily become discouraged and lose our expectation of positive change. We feel powerless and hopeless, and we can't seem to locate the light at the end. Despite God's track record of coming through for us, we often limit Him in what He is able to do. Instead of wanting our own outcome, we need to trust God and His outcome which is the best.

At several points in my life, I have sensed God stretching my faith. Unwelcoming situations, seemingly out of my control, would occur and reoccur. I have seen the lopsided results of handling my difficulties on my own against letting go and letting God manage them. Now that I know with absolute certainty that He will deliver because He has proven it, I will continue to seek God's provision in any unfriendly circumstance, no matter how great or small.

We make decisions and choices every day of our lives. We either live according to our own desires or impulses or live according to the instructions God has given us in His Word. We can follow our own thinking or submit ourselves to the leading of the Holy Spirit who lives within us. Obeying God and walking by faith leads to peace, protection, and limitless blessings. One of His greatest concerns is developing our faith. God moves us from a tentative residency of "I hope it will happen" to an undeniable affirmation of "I know this will happen." He always has good things in store for us. We need to trust Him in the unknown because He is always in control. A faith that cannot be shaken only comes from a faith that has been severely shaken.

The enemy has his plans for evil, but God sees to it that those plans backfire instead, turning them for good in our lives. Many of the obstacles we face, God uses as stepping stones to a greater blessing, concurrently with the completion of His will in our lives. In the midst of finding an escape from our inconvenient situation, we need to draw on God's strength. Refocus and remember His promises. As we continue to put our trust and confidence in Him, He promises to rescue us.

GIANT SLAYERS

"Giants" in our lives can bring to the forefront our hidden strengths. With God's help, we can become Giant Slayers. Take for example the story of David and Goliath. God gave David victory over his giant. Giants will come in many ways. Broadly, it can be anything that stops us from being all God has called us to be, and all He has called us to do. In other words, to stop us from fulfilling our destiny. As a slayer, you'll perceive adverse circumstances as growth; a timely opportunity to gain and not to lose. God is greater than any giant which is why we should never allow fear to overwhelm faith. Fear is the enemy's weapon to paralyze us. Faith is God's weapon to mobilize us. God's promises are greater than any problem and our battle is truly His, not ours. There are many distractions we can fix our eyes on, as many things demand our attention. Discerning and consulting with God before our choices are made, allows us to maintain perfect peace with our decisions.

Whatever storm we are in the midst of, maybe unmet needs, lack of affection, or hurt and pain, God is able to heal us and make us whole. He will enable us to leave the past behind and go forward into the future He has planned for us. Nothing catches Him by surprise, and no scenario is too difficult. His care is tailor-made for us because He knows us so intimately. He knows our weaknesses and He knows our gifts and talents. He helps us with our weaknesses, and if we put our gifts into God's hands we will be surprised to see how He can use them for His glory.

What an amazing option God has granted us as part of our inheritance in Christ. The enablement and empowerment to choose faith over fear. To live lives not dictated by circumstantial evidence, but rather seen through God's sovereign hand of authority over our circumstances. We have the God-granted option of perceiving everything insightfully different, no longer adhering to the common societal approach to life; see it, hear it, and react to it. It is widely understood that walking by sight provides a certain sense of normality to our lives, but it isn't the correct choice. I'm inclined to think if we exercise our option of faith over fear appropriately, we will ultimately lose the desire to fear consistently.

There's a reason why Peter was hesitant to accept Jesus' invitation to walk with Him on the Sea of Galilee. After taking a few steps of success, Peter lost sight of Jesus, adjusted his view to the waves, and down he went. He magnified the circumstances, fear moved in, and Peter sank. While rescuing him, Jesus asks one of the most profound questions ever uttered on the subject matter of faith. "Why did you doubt?" Jesus could have added: The reason you could take one step is the same reason you could have taken as many as you wanted; Me! When you doubted, you didn't doubt yourself, you doubted me!

Faith is the gift of God that enables us to express our praise as loudly in our valleys as on our mountain tops; when conditions are undesirable as when life is going as planned. It is a true test, but one of the pure, gratifying joys of being a believer.

9

This Too Shall Pass

There is a time for everything, and a season for every activity under the heavens. – Ecclesiastes 3:1

Jailed for fighting against apartheid, Nelson Mandela spent twenty-seven years in South African prisons. Throughout those long years, in degrading conditions of abuse and starvation, guards urinated on him and proclaimed, "Here you will die." He never gave up on his dream of a society in which blacks and whites could live in freedom and harmony. And he never stopped hoping that someday he would be released. He later wrote in a prison memoir, "Someday I would once again feel the grass under my feet and walk in the sunshine as a free man." To him, hope meant "keeping one's head pointed toward the sun, one's feet moving forward. There were many dark moments when my faith in humanity was sorely tested, but I would not and could not give myself up to despair." It is a custom in his tribe that grandfathers name their grandchildren, and when his oldest daughter, whom he had not seen for almost two decades, gave birth to a girl, Nelson Mandela named her Azwie—Hope. "The name had special meaning for me," he wrote in his autobiography, *Long Walk to Freedom*, "for during all my years in prison hope never left me and now it never would. I was convinced that this child would be part of a new generation of South Africans for whom apartheid would be a distant memory."

At the age of seventy-one, Nelson Mandela was finally freed and went on to guide South Africa to true democracy, without the wholesale slaughter that residents feared. "I never lost hope that this great transformation would occur," said Mandela. "I always knew that deep down in every human heart, there is mercy and generosity ... Man's goodness is a flame that can be hidden but never extinguished."

The life of Nelson Mandela is one of the greatest examples of the power of patience. With composed persistence, he helped bring about a miracle not only for himself but also for the 43 million others who inhabited South Africa. Under extreme duress, Nelson Mandela was able to tap into something profound in the human spirit: our capacity to hope, which allows us to work patiently toward a goal that we may never see.

When we accept that whatever it is that is driving us silly is going to take as long as it takes to resolve, it is easier to be patient. We surrender to God as time passes, rather than insisting on instant gratification. A baby takes a full nine months to grow in the womb. We don't want them to arrive prematurely. We ought to view the things we are trying to hurry along as unborn babies. How would that affect our capacity to wait?

Why me? Why this? Why now? All of us arrive at these anguished questions at some point. Recognize that your trial may not be a punishment for anything you've done or have not done. If you feel you don't deserve the awful things that are happening to you, consider that this is also applicable to really good things that you've experienced. Do we deserve these any more than we deserve the bad things? When faced with misfortune, instead of asking "Why me?" consider examining "Why not me?" "Why someone else?"

The more we reconcile ourselves to the fact that life moves at its own pace, the more patience we'll have. The kind of patience, which goes far beyond putting up with the momentary irritation of unemployment or someone creating havoc in your life. Waiting patiently asks us to allow life to move through and transform us as we bend like cattails in the wind, twisting and turning yet by God's grace, surviving.

Impatience is often about comparing our present situation to what we think it should be. Things are not going our way or progressing quickly enough. People are not behaving as we think they ought to. This kind of thinking diminishes our capacity for joy, peace, and constructive action. Nothing is perfect—not us, not others, not life. If we can embrace the present moment just as it is, we can better appreciate what a treasure it actually is.

When you stand very close to a painting, it may seem to be composed of random brushstrokes, conflicting colors, and meaningless objects. Take a step back, though, and it all blends together into a meaningful, beautiful image. Such is life, when viewed up close, daily annoyances and nuisances may make no sense whatsoever. But if you step back, and patiently look at the whole picture over time, you are sure to see burdens turned to blessings and chaos turned to meaning—a beautiful display of God's providence.

Burdens weighing you down—family stress, medical issues, overwork—are bound to make you impatient with life's smaller aggravations. Your emotional reserves are dried up, so patience for any new exasperation is in short supply. When you feel overwhelmed, as if suffering is ganging up on you, fall into the arms of God. There you will find unforeseen and untapped strength.

Practice gratitude for all the beauty and blessings in your life. It's a great antidote to discontentment and impatience.

No matter how out of kilter life may seem at the moment, God is with you, actively caring for you, rooting for you, strengthening you—not just watching over you. He wants only the best for us. God created us in love, implanted love within us, and beams love to us at every moment. When we have faith in His loving presence as our guiding principle, then true patience will eclipse all trials.

There is a very great truth that to every disadvantage there is likely a corresponding advantage. Consider the old truism that behind the darkest clouds the sun is shining. In the toughest situations, there is always some value that is inherently good. And if you should not find such value after searching persistently, the positive thinker, by looking for the good, for the advantage, for the sunshine, will come to realize that prevailing to fight another day is the greatest value. What you deeply think and visualize has a strong tendency to produce itself in fact. Make a concerted effort to always think positively, believingly, and expectantly.

PRAY DIFFERENTLY

It is human to doubt and just because we doubt at times, doesn't mean we don't believe. David was the king of lament, expressing his sorrow, fear, doubt, and frustration to God. In fact, over one third of the book of Psalms are qualms of lament, many written by David. David shows us it's okay to struggle with why. And it's okay to express all of your anger, sorrow, and pain before God in your prayers. Your prayer can be a lament and God is pleased with that. When we pour out our hearts before God, no matter what we say, it is a form of worship. Just because we don't feel something in a particular moment doesn't mean our faith foundation is shaken. Sometimes, we need time to catch up. Like David, our lament can turn to praise. When doubt creeps in, we should come boldly before the throne of grace, without shame.

Amid life's challenges, sometimes we have to go deeper and pray for something besides our circumstances. If you're feeling stuck in a place of worry, fear, or pity, there are many ways to pray. Consider targeting God's character and His promises. Pray any prayer in the Bible where someone praises God for who He is, not solely for what He has done (See Psalm 121:1-7). When you are petitioning for a breakthrough, ask the Holy Spirit to shape your prayers.

Keep in mind prayer comes in many flavors: petition, praise and thanksgiving, as well as contemplative, and traditional (like the Our Father). It is good to incorporate all, but each type gives us the wherewithal we need to rise above our daily challenges. See for example the traditional serenity prayer.

God grant me the
Serenity
to accept the things
I cannot change,
Courage to change
the things I can,
and Wisdom to know
the difference.
—*The Serenity Prayer*

Time with God really doesn't have to be complicated or ritualized. Undoubtedly, it's great to have a particular time and place to meet with Him, just as a favorite date location. But a relationship with God is meant for everyday life. Begin wherever you are with a simple prayer. Then simply talk with Him while commuting to work, folding your laundry, or as you enter a difficult season. This daily time is paramount to living an overcomer's life; it will restore everything about you.

FINDING THE GREEN

Some days, our lives feel like we're walking in the lush green pastures of Central Park, and other days feel like we're trekking through the blazing sun of the Sahara Desert. In either scenario, we can choose our focus. We can obsess on the dry and weary ground, or we can look up for small signs of green—shifting our eyes to that which gives us hope and encouragement to press on. There are many sources of "green," and each is a step toward making gratitude part of our journey. Another way to find this form of gratitude is to dwell on what God has done for us in the past. The Israelites serve as a powerful reminder. Throughout the book of Exodus, God repeatedly delivered. From passage on dry ground through the Red Sea, to water from a rock, to quail and manna supplied each day, to rules for living, God provided exactly what His people needed. If our focus is on the daily bread we've already received, we can walk forward in faith and gratitude through our wilderness. In situations or seasons of plenty, it is easy for our hearts to blossom with gratitude. But in the worst circumstances imaginable, we can still focus our attention on that which is true, pure, and admirable. Sometimes, a sliver of green is all we need to keep us going.

Let go and let God work in your life, even if it feels unlivable right now. Remember, God helps in many ways: giving you the strength to endure tough circumstances, comfort in His Word, and you'll even be surprised to see Him preemptively send others into your life to help support you through your difficult time.

Optimism in the face of adversity has always been one of humanity's most powerful traits. And as the world has undergone one of the worst pandemics to date, it is a good time to maintain a healthy amount of optimism. This storm, too, shall pass. Where you're at or where you've been isn't nearly as important as where God wants to take you.

10

Triumph

I can do all this through him who gives me strength.
— Philippians 4:13

Tomorrow always seems to look better than today. Maybe we'll have more money. Maybe we'll find the love of our lives. Maybe we'll shed a few pounds. We spend much of our time waiting for the time to be right, for a special occasion or perfect "today" that we forget to live in the moment that has been assigned to us. We miss out on opportunities for growth while we stand around waiting for life to be delivered to us in a perfect package.

It is easy to believe that we can perform a mindset switch once we get the dream job, the elusive soulmate, or when the weather gets a bit warmer, but there will always be another benchmark. The cycle of waiting to hit one more milestone must end for your life of purpose to begin. Today is accessible, tomorrow isn't promised.

Recondition your minds to make the necessary changes today. The depression you've allowed to become a part of who you are, the individual hindering your progress, the addictive vice you can't seem to shake, end it today. If you've gotten this far in the book, you've certainly already discovered that anything is possible with God. Allow Him residency in your life to help you create the perpetual changes that you desire.

We practice the discipline of surrender when we focus our attention on Jesus. He isn't just the prize at the finish line. He is also the best example of how to run the race. He didn't just design the course of the race. He ran it, and ran it perfectly, relying on and trusting in the Father all along the way. We are to look to Him as the ultimate example of a life of submission.

You need to run the race that God has set before you. Although He has a big design for you, and He knows the details of it, He gives you responsibility for initiative. What is called initiative is faith: We actually get to do something and make decisions, and choices to fulfill what we need to. When we exercise our faith in overcoming life's ups and downs, we synchronously experience peace, and the power of God to undertake any difficulties standing before us.

As you begin to realize that your happiness is a choice, it becomes easier to make decisions about what actions you should take each day. It becomes easier to find positive ways to view the challenges thrown before you. Make it a habit to actively seek out the positive in everything. Remember, prayer serves as our most effective tool here. Revisit Chapter 9 as needed. As we incorporate prayer, the easier it will be to embrace optimism.

Where you are now is a product of your past thoughts and mindset. Equipped with a new perspective, you'll begin to shape today's thoughts to create the life for tomorrow you deserve.

THANKFUL FOR THE SCARS

We have all had experiences that have cut us to the core. Some of these things are our own faults; others aren't. Many of these moments in our lives have left us marked by visible or invisible signs of the past. Someone who has struggled with alcoholism may have inner feelings of shame. An abuse victim may feel loathed. These moments and feelings only mark the beginning of our testimonies; where our wounds become scars.

Scars are simply wounds that are healed. Because they are healed, they no longer carry the pain they once did. They are no longer haunting reminders of a shameful past, but rather evidence of healing and reminders of victory. Our scars tell our stories and have tremendous ability to give hope to those who see or hear of them.

Take Jesus as our pinnacle example. Many observed the gruesome wounds that He suffered during and leading up to His crucifixion at the cross. Upon rising from the dead, Jesus could have appeared with a redeemed body that entirely erased all signs of the past. He could have stepped out of the tomb completely perfect, and people would have marveled at His new body. But Jesus chose to do something much more powerful:

> On the evening of that first day of the week, when the disciples were together, with the doors locked for fear of the Jewish leaders, Jesus came and stood among them and said, "Peace be with you!" After he said this, he showed them his hands and side. The disciples were overjoyed when they saw the Lord. – John 20:19-20

Jesus stood in the room with His disciples and revealed the scars He had gained on the cross. He kept the scars as His testimony, and they tell His story. For those of us who bear deep personal battle scars, let this finest example serve as a reminder to tell our story with undeniable certainty that our scars cannot return as wounds.

TRIED, TRUE, AND TESTED

Within a single seed is the potential for so much new life. Given the proper circumstances, a seed will sprout into a plant, which can then produce more seeds that sprout into more plants. That's a wonderful plan, but it is contingent upon a very uncomfortable process.

When a seed is dropped onto the ground, with the right amount of water, oxygen, and temperature, new life is birthed inside. As water is absorbed into the seed, its outer shell is softened so that when the seed is buried into the proper soil, the shell cracks open and the new life inside can emerge.

Notice that the life held inside of the seed doesn't burst the shell open itself. Rather, the shell is first tried so that new life may arise. Imagine if the seed had never struggled. The potential inside would never be seen, and it would never have the ability to grow.

Do you see the tremendous parallel for your life? As a believer, God plants His seed in you, and new life is birthed. What's holding back your new life? Is it slavery to fear, guilt, doubts? These are the things that the outer shell of the seed represents, which must be cracked and crushed so that all the potential in you can burst forth.

Adversity truly never leaves, and it can walk right through our door at any time. But now, you are equipped with the mental provisions necessary to withstand the roughest periods that you will encounter. With a new zest for life, observe how God turns your disbelief into belief, confusion into clarity, distrust into trust, and losses into wins. Keep Him close and watch Him transform insurmountable circumstances into miraculous successes.

If you feel overburdened or exhausted by the enemy's torment, know this: God's plan always prevails, even in the face of what appears to be a hopeless situation. God is passionate about pursuing you—into the darkest places if He has to—in order to bring you to your desired place. Realize that your calamitous state might be the best tool God has to do some great things in your life. Make an effort today to put Him at the forefront of all your battles. He will begin to present you with victories that you once thought impossible.

When we are aligned with God's will for our lives, it becomes easier to exhibit patience. Because He knows all, we trust Him to answer our insistent petitions with impeccable timing. Recite your favorite biblical promises, trust that God has received your petition, and is truly in control of your situation. Go to Him in prayer and with praise. Acknowledge your fears, confess your weaknesses. Remember, it is through prayer that we receive God's perfect peace that transcends all understanding. We should not hesitate to pray about every matter, good or bad, that develops.

Do recognize that when you pray, you may not always receive the immediate response that you had hoped for. While you wait for an answer, reflect on whether your petition is truly right for the moment. God may first need to strengthen you in certain areas. Use this time to question what He wants from you as your faith is being increased.

Stand today in the truth that you know: God created you; God loves you; God has a plan. Because your existence was crucial, you can trust that He loves you unconditionally enough to see to it that His plan for your life is fulfilled. If you believe these things to be true, don't let up or give up on achieving your life of purpose.

Be encouraged that you can trust Him to see you through whatever challenges life throws at you. And, if you still haven't received what you are praying for, consider that God is likely working on something bigger and better. My prayer is that the words in this book offer timely strength and reassurance when you need it most.

What you behold is what you desire. Whatever you dwell on is what you will become. Refrain from committing your thoughts to anything else than what God has promised He will do for you. Now, applying this approach with a faith that has been fortified through your struggles, rest assured you will achieve your triumph.

Affirmations for When You Feel

AFRAID

God is our refuge and strength, an ever-present help in trouble. – Psalm 46:1

Be strong and courageous. Do not be afraid or terrified because of them, for the Lord your God goes with you; he will never leave you nor forsake you. – Deuteronomy 31:6

ANXIOUS

Do not be anxious about anything, but in every situation, by prayer and petition, with thanksgiving, present your requests to God. And the peace of God, which transcends all understanding, will guard your hearts and your minds in Christ Jesus. – Philippians 4:6-7

Cast all your anxiety on him because he cares for you. Be alert and of sober mind. Your enemy the devil prowls around like a roaring lion looking for someone to devour. – 1 Peter 5:7-8

ASHAMED

If we confess our sins, he is faithful and just and will forgive us our sins and purify us from all unrighteousness. – 1 John 1:9

You will again have compassion on us; you will tread our sins underfoot and hurl all our iniquities into the depths of the sea. – Micah 7:19

BROKEN-HEARTED

He heals the brokenhearted and binds up their wounds. – Psalm 147:3

The Lord is close to the brokenhearted and saves those who are crushed in spirit. – Psalm 34:18

DEPRESSED

The Lord is a refuge for the oppressed, a stronghold in times of trouble. – Psalm 9:9

I waited patiently for the Lord; he turned to me and heard my cry. He lifted me out of the slimy pit, out of the mud and mire; he set my feet on a rock and gave me a firm place to stand. – Psalm 40:1-2

DISAPPOINTED

Forget the former things; do not dwell on the past. – Isaiah 43:18

For I know the plans I have for you," declares the Lord, "plans to prosper you and not to harm you, plans to give you hope and a future. – Jeremiah 29:11

DISCOURAGED

Though you have made me see troubles, many and bitter, you will restore my life again; from the depths of the earth you will again bring me up. – Psalm 71:20

Finally, brothers and sisters, whatever is true, whatever is noble, whatever is right, whatever is pure, whatever is lovely, whatever is admirable—if anything is excellent or praiseworthy—think about such things. – Philippians 4:8

DOUBTFUL

Now faith is confidence in what we hope for and assurance about what we do not see. – Hebrews 11:1

And without faith it is impossible to please God, because anyone who comes to him must believe that he exists and that he rewards those who earnestly seek him. – Hebrews 11:6

HOPELESS

Trust in the Lord with all your heart and lean not on your own understanding; in all your ways submit to him, and he will make your paths straight. – Proverbs 3:5-6

But those who hope in the Lord will renew their strength. They will soar on wings like eagles; they will run and not grow weary, they will walk and not be faint. – Isaiah 40:3

IMPATIENT

Wait for the Lord; be strong and take heart and wait for the Lord. – Psalm 27:14

Be joyful in hope, patient in affliction, faithful in prayer. – Romans 12:12

JEALOUS

A heart at peace gives life to the body, but envy rots the bones. – Proverbs 14:30

When you ask, you do not receive, because you ask with wrong motives, that you may spend what you get on your pleasures. – James 4:3

LONELY

Though my father and mother forsake me, the Lord will receive me. – Psalm 27:10

When you pass through the waters, I will be with you; and when you pass through the rivers, they will not sweep over you. When you walk through the fire, you will not be burned; the flames will not set you ablaze. – Isaiah 43:2

OVERWHELMED

Come to me, all you who are weary and burdened, and I will give you rest. – Matthew 11:28

The Lord will fight for you; you need only to be still. – Exodus 14:14

STRESSED

Cast your cares on the Lord and he will sustain you; he will never let the righteous be shaken. –Psalm 55:22

Consider it pure joy, my brothers and sisters, whenever you face trials of many kinds, because you know that the testing of your faith produces perseverance. – James 1:2-3

TEMPTED

Do not conform to the pattern of this world, but be transformed by the renewing of your mind. Then you will be able to test and approve what God's will is—his good, pleasing and perfect will. – Romans 12:2

No temptation has overtaken you except what is common to mankind. And God is faithful; he will not let you be tempted beyond what you can bear. But when you are tempted, he will also provide a way out so that you can endure it. – 1 Corinthians 10:13

UNLOVED

Can a mother forget the baby at her breast and have no compassion on the child she has borne? Though she may forget, I will not forget you! – Isaiah 49:15

Because of the Lord's great love we are not consumed, for his compassions never fail. – Lamentations 3:22

UPSET

Fools give full vent to their rage, but the wise bring calm in the end. – Proverbs 29:11

A gentle answer turns away wrath, but a harsh word stirs up anger. – Proverbs 15:1

Acknowledgments

This book is a team effort, and the result of a collaboration of gifts and motivation from an amazing group of individuals.

I want to begin by acknowledging my mom, Patricia Felix, for my Christian upbringing, and consistent support in all of my personal aspirations. One of my major motivations for writing this book was to be a pillar of support to others as she has always been for me.

I also would like to thank ALCC Winners House for welcoming me with open arms into your loving church family. Your warmth sparked a renewed energy within me on my journey to walk closer with God.

I also want to thank Vide Press, who believed in my message, championed this book, and fought to get it into the hands of as many people as possible.

I also want to acknowledge Sully Guzman, for being one of my most selfless, and God-fearing friends. A book you gifted to me, ultimately inspired me to write *Triumph*.

Finally, to every friend, foe, acquaintance and mentor that I have ever crossed paths with—thank you for contributing to my experiences. You are all diversely instrumental in my decision to write and publish this book.

Notes

Barton, Ruth Haley. *https://www.christianitytoday.com/.* 28 June 2012.

Casey, Karen. *All We Have Is All We Need: Daily Steps Toward a Peaceful Life.* York Beach: Conari Press, 2006.

Daniels, Dr. Dharius. *Relational Intelligence: The People Skills You Need For the Life of Purpose You Want.* Dallas: Zondervan, 2020.

David, Susan and Christina Congleton. "Managing Yourself." *Emotional Agility* November 2013.

Laaser, Dr. Mark R. *Healing the Wounds of Sexual Addiction.* Grand Rapids: Zondervan, 2004.

Lucado, Max. *Anxious for Nothing: Finding Calm in a Chaotic World.* Nashville: Thomas Nelson, 2017.

MacArhur, John. *christianity.com.* 12 January 2021. 8 April 2021.

Mandela, Nelson. *Long Walk to Freedom.* Boston: Little, Brown and Company, 1994.

Mills, James P. *God's Rx for Fear and Worry.* Lake Mary: Siloam, 2019.

Moody, Van. *The People Factor: How Building Great Relationships and Ending Bad Ones Unlocks Your God-Given Purpose.* Nashville: Thomas Nelson, 2014.

Odessky, Dr. Helen. *Stop Anxiety from Stopping You: The Breakthrough Program for Panic & Social Anxiety.* Coral Gables: Mango Publishing Group, 2017.

Paprocki, Joe. *A Well-Built Faith: A Catholic's Guide to Knowing and Sharing What We Believe.* Chicago: Loyola Press, 2008.

Price, Richard. *Tacoma Christian Counseling.* 09 Dec 2019. 2021.

Thomas, Gary. *When to Walk Away: Finding Freedom from Toxic People.* Grand Rapids: Zondervan, 2019.

Thomas, Paul and Jennifer Margulis. *The Addiction Spectrum: A Compassionate, Holistic Approach to Recovery.* New York: HarperCollins, 2018.

Veith Jr., Gene Edward. *Post-Christian: A Guide to Contemporary Thought and Culture.* Wheaton: Crossway, 2020.

Westerbeck, Zachary. *You're Not Alone: The Only Book You'll Ever Need to Overcome Anxiety and Depression.* Middletown: Reading List Editorial, 2020.

Whybrow, Peter. *Why We Must Kick Our Addiction to Electronic Cocaine.* London, 13 July 2012. Website.

CPSIA information can be obtained
at www.ICGtesting.com
Printed in the USA
BVHW042137280622
640817BV00010B/490